Birds in the Land of the Bible

Photography: **Yossi Eshbol**
Text: **Uzi Paz**

In cooperation with the Society for Protection of Nature, Israel.

© PALPHOT Ltd.

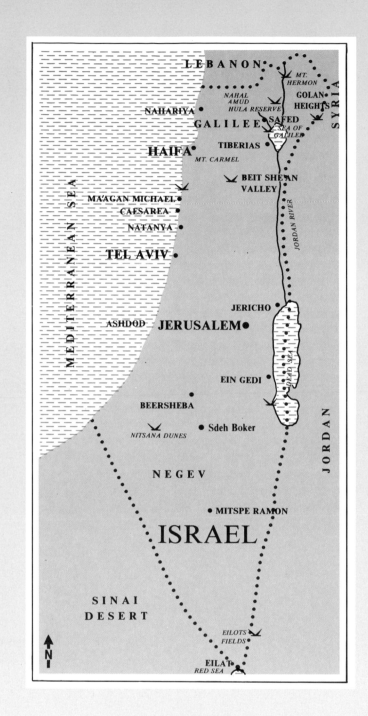

Printed by Israphot, Karney Shomron
Designed by F. Klevitsky

Produced by Palphot Ltd.,
P.O.Box 2, Herzlia 46100, Israel.
Tel. 052-555238, Telex: 33884, Fax: 052-571701.
ISBN 965-280-064-3
Cat. No. 44051
PUBLISHED BY PALPHOT LTD.

I N T R O D U C T I O N

The Jewish sages said, The Land of Israel is at the center of the world, and Jerusalem is at the center of the Land of Israel. This was also the viewpoint of the Crusaders. One expression of these views is a map which was drawn at the end of the 16th century. The map depicts the world in the form of a trefoil centering on Jerusalem. Jerusalem marks the junction between Europe, Asia and Africa. For birds, this map is not imaginary. Israel is indeed a crossroads for birds from distant lands. They come from all points of the compass: northern Europe, the shores of the Mediterranean Sea, the steppes of Asia, Siberia, the Indian subcontinent, tropical Africa and the Sahara desert. The Mediterranean shores of Israel also witness marine birds coming from the west, where the open sea stretches and joins the oceans.

Bünting, The World in the the Shape of a Clover-Leaf with Jerusalem as the Center.
By courtesy of the National and University Library, Jerusalem.

Thus, for example, we can watch the Turnstone and the Red-throated Pipit, which hail from the Arctic region in the far north; the Spur-winged Plover and the Namaqua Dove from sub-Saharan tropical Africa; the Spotted Redshank and the Fieldfare, from Siberia; the Desert Lark and the Spotted Sandgrouse from the Sahara. The Bluethroat and the Jay are widely distributed over the temperate zones of Europe and Asia. The Yellow-vented Bulbul and the Graceful Warbler, on the other hand, come from the tropical regions of Asia and Africa. Black-eared Wheatear and Sardinian Warbler are distributed only in the Mediterranean basin. Upcher's Warbler and Isabelline Wheatear come from the steppes of central and western Russia (the Irano-Turanian zone). Black Francolin and White-breasted Kingfisher originate in tropical Asia, while Leach's Petrel and Gannet may stray in from the vast Atlantic Ocean. On the other hand, Israel is also the place to see birds that are distributed all over the world, such as Great White Egret and Barn Owl. Alongside these species, birds limited to the eastern regions of the Mediterranean Sea are also visible: Syrian Woodpecker, Masked Shrike and Cretszchmar's Bunting. Other subspecies are found only in Israel and its immediate surroundings, such as Palestine Sunbird and Sinai Rosefinch.

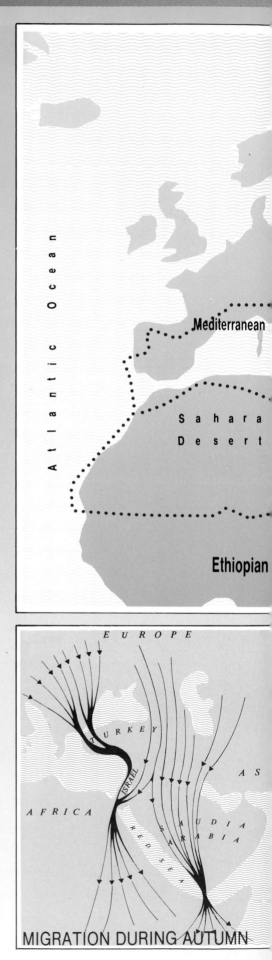

MIGRATION DURING AUTUMN

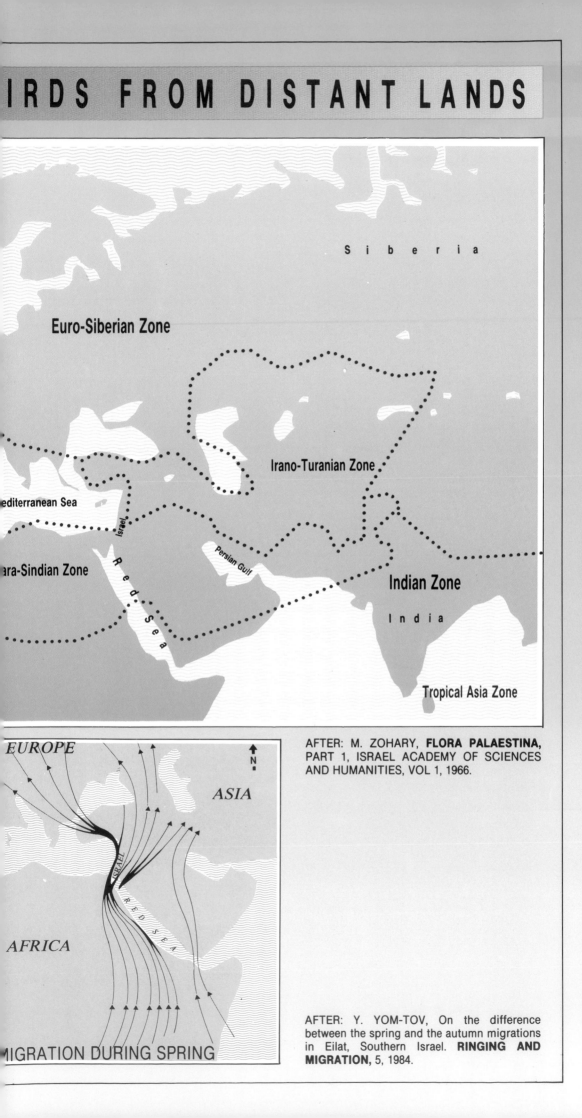

S i b e r i a

Euro-Siberian Zone

Irano-Turanian Zone

editerranean Sea

Israel

ara-Sindian Zone

R e d   S e a

Persian Gulf

Indian Zone

I n d i a

Tropical Asia Zone

AFTER: M. ZOHARY, **FLORA PALAESTINA,** PART 1, ISRAEL ACADEMY OF SCIENCES AND HUMANITIES, VOL 1, 1966.

EUROPE

ASIA

N

ISRAEL

RED SEA

AFRICA

IGRATION DURING SPRING

AFTER: Y. YOM-TOV, On the difference between the spring and the autumn migrations in Eilat, Southern Israel. **RINGING AND MIGRATION,** 5, 1984.

his is the basis for understanding why such a small country, with an area of only 31,000 square kilometers — about one-eighth of the area of England, or 1/300 part of the United States — is the place to see about 500 different bird species. This is about the same number of the bird species known in England, and only 150 less than the total number of bird species in the United States. Indeed, Israel has a very wide and varied range of bird life.

However, geographical location is hardly sufficient to explain these riches. The climatic variety of the country is another contributing factor. In the north, Israel's "head" rests on the snows of Mount Hermon, while in the south its "feet" dabble in the tropical waters of the Gulf of Eilat. Upper Galilee has an average annual rainfall of 800-1000 millimeters, while in most of the Negev area annual rainfall reaches an average of only 25 millimeters. The climate along the shore of the Mediterranean is temperate and comfortable for most of the year, while the climate in the Rift Valley section is warmer, especially along the Dead Sea and the Arava valleys.

Israel also enjoys a great variety of landscapes and habitats: seashore and "sea" of sands; some remnants of swamps and much more recent fishponds; farmlands and meadows; natural woods and afforested areas; broad plains and tall cliffs; rocky landscapes and hamada expanses. All these widely differing features join to form a whole country.

Tiny Israel is indeed wealthy. Each of these landscapes makes it possible for a different variety of bird life to flourish. In addition to all these features, the annual phenomenon of migration must be borne in mind. This is one of the most impressive and important processes in the life cycle of many birds. Some 250 species migrate south in the fall from Europe and Asia, to spend the winter in Africa. They retrace their path in the spring. Most populations of migrating birds, which breed in eastern and central Europe as well as in western Asia, are very noticeable as they fly through Israel.

The country offers a place to rest for the small songbirds, before or after they cross the vast Sahara Desert. Sometimes, especially during the spring migration, they are so exhausted that they may be approached at quite close range, and can even be photographed without special efforts or techniques. However, only a small proportion of these bird populations passes through Israel. Most of them fly over the Mediterranean and across the Red Sea, taking the shorter and more direct route. On the other hand, the soaring birds such as Raptors, as well as Storks and Pelicans, must pass through Israel en route to Africa or on their way back. These birds carry out most of their journey by soaring and gliding. They must therefore bypass expanses of open sea and large lakes, even if this lengthens their route. Conditions for soaring are non-existent over seas and lakes. Thus, almost the entire population of these species finds its way through Israel. Among these, for example, are Pelicans, Storks and Raptors such as Lesser Spotted Eagles and Buzzards. In the fall, on their way south, they fly around the eastern part of the Mediterranean. Flying north in the spring, they must bypass the Red Sea and its northern sections (the Gulf of Eilat and the Gulf of Suez); thus, they cross over the Negev, or gather at the northern tip of the Gulf of Eilat. The favorable soaring conditions in Israel, especially along the line of the Syrian-African Rift, enhance bird migration along that route. Israel is considered one of the best places in the world to watch bird migration. This phenomenon was a source of wonder for the ancients: "Yea, the stork in the heavens knoweth her appointed times; and the turtle and the swallow and the crane" (Jeremiah, 8:7). It is in fact difficult to remain indifferent to the spectacle of migration when the performers are about 250,000 Storks, 140,000 Lesser Spotted Eagles and 500,000 Honey Buzzards. These birds join millions of others, which are less prominent as they fly over.

The birds of Israel are usually divided into five groups, depending on the seasons when they can be seen in the country: residents, summer visitors, winter visitors, migrants, and vagrants. Accordingly, we have divided this booklet into five sections. In each section, we have emphasized the species that characterise the unique zoo-geographic crossroads that the country forms. Most of these species are never seen by the birdwatchers in western and central Europe.

RESIDENT BIRDS

Resident birds are those that live in Israel all year round: summer and winter, spring and fall. They do not take part in the drama of migration. This group numbers about 100 species, including large birds such as Griffon Vulture and Golden Eagle as well as small birds such as Wren and Palestine Sunbird; common birds such as Yellow-vented Bulbul and Blackbird, as well as rare ones such as Lammergeier and Negev Lappet-faced Vulture. Some of them live all year round in the same territory; among these are Graceful Warbler and Eagle Owl. Others gather in flocks in the fall and rove around, like Goldfinch and Corn Bunting. Resident birds also include many social species which live in a group all year round, such as Rock Dove and Cattle Egret. They roam and feed in flocks and sleep and nest in permanent colonies.

Although resident species constitute only about 20% of Israel's birds, they amount to about 40% of all the species in this booklet. In the long run, it is they who give a special character to Israel's avifauna.

Black-winged Stilt, *Himantopus himantopus*

The **House Sparrow** is known today in most parts of the world; it became distributed in some areas through the agency of man. Therefore, it does not merit special mention here, although it is probably the most common bird in Israel, mainly in settled regions. However, even the most congested cities offer sightings of other species not familiar to the European or American visitor.

House Sparrow, *Passer domesticus*

The **Yellow-vented Bulbul** is probably the most noticeable of Israel's resident birds. This large, long-tailed songbird has a distinctive black head and sulphur-yellow under-tail coverts. It is distributed in the region between southern Turkey and Oman. Most of its relatives sound their calls all over tropical Asia, and only a few in Africa.

The Yellow-vented Bulbul is fond of singing. The name Bulbul is derived from Arabic and means "singer". Yellow-vented Bulbuls usually live in pairs. The bird feeds mainly on various types of fruit, and sometimes causes damage to orchards of loquats, apricots, dates and guava pears. Where food is plentiful, the birds will gather in a clamorous group that can number dozens of individuals. The eggs are an unusual lilac color.

Yellow-vented Bulbul, *Pycnonotus xanthopygos*

9

Palestine Sunbird, *Nectarina osea*

While the Yellow-vented Bulbul prefers to stay among the branches of a tree or a large bush, the **Palestine Sunbird** prefers blooming bushes or even garden flowers. The Palestine Sunbird is tiny, with a delicate, long, curving bill. It is fond of hovering before flowers from which it sips nectar. The female is brownish-gray, with a black tail. The male is a shiny black, with iridescent shades of green and violet on the head and breast. In shape and behavior, the Palestine Sunbird resembles the hummingbirds of South America; however, the species are not related. The Palestine Sunbird is the only representative of its family in Israel. The family is distributed all over the tropical regions of the Old World — Africa, Asia and Australia. Israel's Palestine Sunbirds are the most northerly of any member of the family. They are found in Israel and its neighboring countries: southern Lebanon, Jordan, Sinai, and the western and southern coasts of Arabia. Up to the early 20th century, Palestine Sunbird was extremely rare in Israel, and was found almost exclusively in desert oases. Since then, the species has expanded its range considerably, probably due to the increase in ornamental gardens in which nectar-producing flowers are plentiful. Nowadays the bird is common, and sometimes even nests at the entrance to a house or in a pot plant on a balcony. Like other birds of tropical regions, where snakes are common, the Palestine Sunbird hangs its pear-shaped nest on a hanging branch or creeper tendril.

Another bird which often nests in attics, on window-ledges and in pot plants on balconies is the reddish-brown **Palm Dove**. The Palm Dove comes from the tropical regions of Africa. According to one common view, Israel's Palm-Dove population is

Palm Dove, *Streptopelia senegalensis*

derived from birds introduced to mosques by local Muslims, since they were fond of its distinctive cooing call. In any case, at the turn of the 20th century Palm Doves were known only around mosques in Jerusalem, Gaza, Jaffa and Ramle. The species began to spread from these locations, and its range has expanded considerably since the 1930s. By the end of the 1960s it was considered common all over the country: in cities and towns as well as in fruit-tree orchards, woods and forests. In the spring, its cooing is heard from dawn all day long, even in downtown city areas.

Open areas bordering on towns and settlements are a good place to see pairs of a large plover, its contrasting colors resembling the dress of a waiter. This is the **Spur-winged Plover**, which originates in the savannah areas south of the Sahara Desert. Nowadays, Spur-winged Plovers are so common along Israel's roads and fields — their nests are even found in barnyards — that it is hard to believe that they were quite rare in the country as late as 1963.

On winter evenings, large numbers of Spur-winged Plovers may congregate in fields where crops are grown under plastic sheeting. Perhaps this provides them with a a warmer environment.

Spur-winged Plover, *Hoplopterus spinosus*

Cattle Egret, *Bubulcus ibis*

Garbage dumps and fields, especially near grazing herds of cattle and flocks of sheep, are the setting for **Cattle Egret**. The birds accompany the cows and the sheep, waiting for them to flush insects from the grass. The Cattle Egrets then pluck them out of the air with their bills.

Cattle Egrets only arrived in Israel from Africa in the early 1950s. However, they adjusted very well to this country, and dozens of nesting colonies now exist everywhere. Each of these colonies may number hundreds or even thousands of pairs. For some reason these colonies are often located within settlements of all types: kibbutz, moshav, town or city.

Visitors around grazing areas can also see the quick movements of the **Graceful Warbler**. It skips and hops about, occasionally fluttering its wings and cocking its tail. This tiny bird weighs only about 7 grams. It is distributed from the Horn of Africa to the plains of the Ganges River in India, and northwards to southern Turkey. It is quite common in Israel's gardens, meadows and farmlands. Its distinctive call is heard everywhere in these habitats. Graceful Warblers live in regular pairs on permanent territories no larger than half an acre.

Graceful Warbler, *Prinia gracilis*

Calandra Lark, *Melanocorypha calandra*

Meadows as well as farmlands are also the home of the **Calandra Lark**. This largest of Israel's Larks weighs about 55 grams, and has a distinctive black ring around its neck. It is distributed all over the Mediterranean basin and east to the steppes of central Asia. During most of the year it flocks and joins other Lark species and Starlings. In the nesting season it lives in pairs, on territories. Its summer diet consists mainly of insects; in the winter it feeds on shoots and leaves.

Kingfishers are well known as birds which are linked with bodies of water and live on small fish and various water insects. It is therefore a surprise to encounter **White-breasted Kingfisher** far away from any sources of water: in gardens, irrigated fields and sparsely planted orchards. However, it can also subsist on a diet of mole-crickets, grasshoppers, crabs and various reptiles. It sometimes even catches other birds.

White-breasted Kingfisher originates in tropical Asia, and ranges west to Turkey. Like all kingfishers, it nests in burrows which it digs in vertical banks of river, fish-pond or pit.

Another Kingfisher resident in Israel is the **Pied Kingfisher**. It is often seen hovering over the waters of the Sea of Galilee and the blue expanses of fishponds. Pied Kingfisher is another representative of tropical fauna in Israel. The species is distributed over Africa as well as in southeastern Asia. It feeds primarily on fish. Unlike most Kingfishers, which live solitary lives, the Pied Kingfisher is social. Several individuals are often seen together. In some areas, such as Nahal HaTaninim stream, near the fishponds of Ma'agan Michael, dozens of Pied Kingfishers gather on tamarisk trees to spend the night together in winter.

White-breasted Kingfisher, *Halcyon smyrnensis*

Pied Kingfisher, *Ceryle rudis*

Marbled Teal, *Mamaronetta angustirostris*

Israel's fishponds have their finest hour in winter. Tens of thousands of birds, members of about 80 different species, then gather at these bodies of water. In summer, the ponds are more like blue deserts! Only a few bird species nest in Israel. One of these is the **Marbled Teal** — a duck which is quite rare in other parts of the world. It breeds only in limited areas, such as the Mediterranean basin and western Asia. This duck is different from most other duck species in that the sexes look alike; nor are there seasonal changes of color. Marbled Teals are found almost exclusively in the Hula Valley, particularly in the Hula Nature Reserve.

Some members of the Warbler family nest in the thick growths of reed and papyrus around Israel's fishponds and in the few surviving swamps. The largest of these species is the **Clamorous Reed Warbler**. It is distributed over southern Asia, Australia and along the Nile Valley. In Israel, Clamorous Reed Warblers live in every reed thicket, from the Hula Valley to the Eilat region. During the nesting season, Clamorous Reed Warblers perch on the tops of reeds and sound their throaty calls. The nest, resembling a deep basket, is attached to the reeds and sways with the wind.

Clamorous Reed Warbler, *Acrocephalus stentoreus*

Sardinian Warbler, *Sylvia melanocephala*

Where the valleys and plains blend into the foothills, and wherever bushes dominate the sparse maquis landscape, the **Sardinian Warbler** finds a home. This is the commonest of Israel's resident Warblers. It is easily distinguished by the red ring around its eye. This Warbler is distributed all around the Mediterranean. During most of the year it hides in the bushes and is quite difficult to spot. However, both members of the pair communicate by hoarse calls at short intervals.

Israel's maquis areas are the home of three very common species: Blackbird, Jay and Syrian Woodpecker. Until not too long ago, these three species were found only in natural maquis areas. In recent years their range has expanded considerably, in the wake of orange groves which form an artificial "maquis" area. These birds now can be seen almost throughout the country.

The Jay is widely distributed in the world, over most of Europe and large parts of Asia. There are many subspecies in this range. The Israeli subspecies is *Garrulus glandarius atricapillus,* with a distinctive black cap. It is distributed from southern Turkey to southern Iran.

Jays are not particular about their food. They also rob eggs or chicks out of bird nests. Therefore, jays are often mobbed by birds calling loudly, to "stop the thief".

The **Syrian Woodpecker** originated on the east coast of the Mediterranean. Over the last hundred years its distribution area has expanded greatly. By 1951 it had reached Austria. In Israel, Syrian Woodpeckers adapted to modern innovations, and discovered plastic water pipes which they began to peck until holes were created. In one case they pecked at plastic-covered telephone cables, cutting off lines to an entire village.

Syrian Woodpecker, *Dendrocopus syriacus*

Chukar, *Alectoris chucar*

Hill regions where the maquis has been cut down and the landscape is rocky and dry are the home of the **Long-billed Pipit**. This large Pipit resembles the Wagtail in shape, and the Lark in coloring. It is distributed from Kashmir in northern India to South Africa. It usually lives in pairs, on rather large territories (about 20 acres) in the rainier parts of Israel. In winter, Long-billed Pipits roam in small groups, and may reach Israel's large valleys. The nest is in a small depression which the female hollows out underneath a rock. This Pipit is the main host of European Cuckoos in Israel. The country is one of the only two areas in the world where these two species meet (the other area is northern India).

Rock cliffs are the stronghold of raptors. Here they find protection during their long breeding season. Their dependence on the cliff is so complete that for many species the climatic factor becomes secondary. Thus, we can see raptors nesting in northern Israel as well as in the desert. One of these species is the Griffon Vulture.

The **Griffon Vulture** is one of Israel's largest raptors. It spends long periods in the air, soaring without a wing-beat, with only its white head moving from side to side. Griffon Vultures feed on carcasses, and they function as sanitation crews, cleaning out the area. Griffon Vultures were formerly quite

Griffon Vulture, *Gyps fulvus*

common all over Israel. Nowadays, they are very rare. The cliffs of Nahal Ammud in Galilee and Nahal Daliyot in the Golan are the best and most comfortable sites for watching them. They nest on rock-ledges. The female lays a single egg, and both parents incubate it for about 54 days. They then feed the chick in the nest for about three months. Griffon Vultures are distributed from Spain to the Himalayas. The bird is mentioned in the Bible 26 times and symbolizes power, speed and lightness of movement.

Flocks of **Chukar** are visible all over Israel, including the expanses of the Negev, farm fields, orchards and sandy areas. This was not always the case. A 19th-century zoologist who traveled over the country stated: "Chukars have never been found in plains or grainfields, but only on rocky hills." They have spread due to the disappearance of the predators and raptors which used to prey on them. These hunters were poisoned as an indirect result of pesticides used against field voles (which endangered crops) and jackals (which spread rabies).

Chukars are distributed from Turkey to eastern China. Israel has two subspecies. The northerly one *(Alectoris chukar cypriotes)* is large and dark, while A. C. Sinaica, in the Negev and Sinai, are smaller, and lighter-colored.

The Chukar introduces us to the desert regions of Israel. About 50 bird species breed in these regions, most of them residents. A smaller, lighter "version" of the Chukar is the **Sand Partridge**, of which the prophet Jeremiah said, "As the partridge that broodeth over young which she hath not brought forth..." (17:11). Sand Partridges are restricted in range to the region east of the Nile, the deserts of Sinai and of Israel, and the coasts of Arabia to Oman.

Sand Partridge, *Ammoperdix heyi*

Long-billed Pipit, *Anthus similis*

Except during the nesting season, Sand Partridges gather in groups of 10-20 individuals. When the rainy season begins, the group separates into pairs. The male then sounds his call from perches on stones, rocks and other prominent observation points.

The Sand Partridge is camouflaged by coloring which blends in almost completely with the desert background. It is quite difficult to locate and notice a Sand Partridge "frozen" in one position. Sand Partridges, like Chukars, spend a great deal of time on foot. They usually use their wings only when they are in distress.

thick, bright orange bill, especially during the nesting season. The male then perches on rocks and sounds a trumpet-like call, which gives it its common name. During other seasons, the birds group and roam in flocks sometimes numbering scores of individuals. Trumpeter Finches are best seen near the few water sources of the Negev. Since they feed on seeds, water must be available.

The **Sinai Rosefinch** has a far more restricted range. The subspecies which breeds in Israel is limited to the southern Negev, Sinai and the areas between Jordan and Arabia. Three other subspe-

Hume's Tawny Owl, *Strix butleri*

The coloring of **Hume's Tawny Owl** also blends in with the desert background. This owl is considered very rare. Its range is similar to that of the Sand Partridge: from east of the Nile to Arabia; it is also found further east, to southern Pakistan. Very little is known about its frequency throughout this range, as well as about its diet, behavior, or breeding biology. The fence around the Ein Gedi Field Study Center of the Society for the Protection of Nature in Israel seems to offer the best conditions and highest likelihood in the world for observing this rare bird.

A pinkish tint sometimes enhances the camouflage coloring of desert birds. This is the case with the **Trumpeter Finch**. Besides the pink tinge which the male takes on, they are distinguished by a

Sinai Rosefinch, *Carpodacus synoicus*

Trumpeter Finch, *Bucanetes githagineus*

cies of this Rosefinch are found in Afghanistan and China. In the spring, the male is colored a strong pink. In the fall, after the change of feathers, its brown color seems quite ordinary. The lovely rose color is noticeable again only after the feather tips become abraded. Sinai Rosefinches can be seen at Ein Netafim — a tiny trickling spring near Eilat — where they come to drink all year round. In winter, they also gather at the campground near the Amram Pillars, where they feed on food scraps.

Other birds which are totally dependent on a water source, although they are desert species,

are Sandgrouse. Five sandgrouse species live in the Negev. In the fall and winter flocks numbering thousands of individuals can be seen in the fields of the western Negev. However, the best place to watch them is in a gully near Eilat, where a small trough near the Eilat water reservoir attracts dozens of **Lichtenstein Sandgrouse** every day at dusk. They arrive in complete silence, landing at some distance from the water. If they are not alarmed, they walk quickly to the trough. They drink and stay at the spot for a while. Finally, they bow to each other, as if giving a signal to take wing, and disappear into the dark.

Lichtenstein Sandgrouse, *Pterocles lichtensteinii*

21

Other desert birds include black among their colors, displaying a stark contrast with the colors of their environment. Since black is also heat-absorbent, it is actually surprising to find this combination among desert birds. Among the black birds are Brown-necked Raven and the smaller Fan-tailed Raven. While the Brown-necked Raven originates in the Saharo-Sindian desert zone, the

Another black bird is **Tristram's Grackle**, which also originates in tropical Africa. At first glimpse it resembles a Blackbird; but its behavior is that of a Starling, and it is usually found in groups. It has characteristic calls: its song is melodious and flute-like, and the communicating cries between individuals in the group are also distinctive. In flight, a chestnut patch on the wing becomes

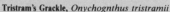

Tristram's Grackle, *Onychognthus tristramii*

smaller Fan-tailed Raven comes from the Horn of Africa. The Brown-necked Raven usually lives in pairs, throughout the Negev and the Judean Desert. The Fan-tailed Raven, on the other hand, lives in flocks, mainly along the Arava Valley. It is a superb aerial acrobat, and seems to enjoy stunts on the wing.

visible. The bird is named for the British canon Henry Baker Tristram, who visited Israel in the mid-19th century and is considered the father of Israeli zoology. Tristram's Grackles are limited in distribution mainly to the Arava Valley, although in recent years the species has expanded its range. It feeds on various fruits, and thus sometimes causes damage to farmers.

Other birds which are noticeable in the desert thanks to their black coloring — though they are much smaller than ravens or even Tristram's grackles — are the various species of Wheatears. One of the commonest and most noticeable of these is the White-crowned Black Wheatear. This Wheatear lives in pairs in canyons in the Judean Desert and along cliffs of the rift valley. The rocky slopes throughout the desert are the home of the **Mourning Wheatear,** while the plateaus are populated by the Desert Wheatear. White-crowned Black Wheatears prefer to perch on rocks and large prominent stones, surveying the vicinity and searching for insects from this vantage point. Its distribution area extends from western Sahara up to Saudi-Arabia.

Mourning Wheatear, *Oenanthe lugens*

The **Blackstart** is related to the Wheatears. It often flutters and spreads its black tail, as though to justify its name. It originates in the savannah region south of the Sahara. In Israel, it lives in territorial pairs, mainly in areas with concentrations of acacia trees throughout the Negev, the Arava Valley and the Judean Desert. Unlike most birds, which quickly flee from man, Blackstarts are not especially nervous around people. They can often be tempted to come up by scattering bits of bread.

Blackstart, *Cercomela melanura*

SUMMER VISITORS

Summer visitors comprise about 60 species. These are birds which nest and raise their brood in Israel, and migrate to their winter homes in the fall. Most of them fly south to Africa, except for the Black-headed Bunting: it migrates eastward, to spend the winter in northwestern India.

Summer visitors begin to return to Israel from their wintering grounds as early as February. The first Egyptian vultures arrive in mid-February. Swifts always re-appear in the last week of February. However, most of the summer visitors return in March. Among them are Cretszchmar's Bunting, Masked Shrike, Upcher's Warbler, and Whitethroat. Others wait for April, such as Common Tern and Black-headed Bunting.

Swifts begin making their way south as early as late June. Lesser Kestrels, as well as Collared Pratincoles and House Martins, start migrating in July. Most summer residents migrate in September, but some tarry until October, such as Hobbies and Red-rumped Swallows.

Many individuals of summer visitors species also pass through Israel, en route to and from their nesting areas in more northerly regions.

Rufous Bush Robin, *Cercotrichas galactotes*

Blackeared Wheatear, *Oenanthe hispanica*

Israel has 11 species of Wheatears, 8 of which nest in this country. Each species lives in a different habitat. The commonest of all is **Black-eared Wheatear**. This Wheatear nests in rocky, dissected areas throughout the mountains and hills of northern and central Israel. Its range is typically Mediterranean, although it penetrates the steppes of western Asia — the Irano-Turanian region — to a certain extent. It can be seen in spring, passing overhead in small, sparse flocks. Its black and white tail provides distinctive identification. The migrants soon pass out of sight, and only nesting pairs remain in Israel. The Black-eared Wheatear is an active bird, constantly in motion inside its territory, and is therefore easy to spot and watch.

While the Black-eared Wheatear prefers rocky, bare mountainous areas, the **Rufous Bush Robin** lives in fruit-tree orchards and gardens in plains and valleys. In this bird, as well, the tail is an unmistakeable identifying feature. From time to time, the bird cocks its tail, fan-like, displaying the rufous-chestnut color with black and white spots at the edges. Rufous Bush Robins are very territorial and may attack songbirds of other species which stray into their territory. Their range is Mediterranean — Irano-Turanian, but representatives of the species are also found in the savannas of tropical Africa. It nests in shadowy spots, sometimes even in barrels, boxes or abandoned farming machinery. The nest lining often contains a snakeskin. In fact, a nest with a snakeskin is quite likely to be that of a Rufous Bush Robin.

Orphean Warbler, *Sylvia hortensis*

Unlike the two previous species, the **Orphean Warbler** returns in summer to natural woodlands, in the Samaria hills, Mount Carmel and Galilee, and in the northern part of Israel in the foothills of Mount Hermon. However, during the spring and fall migration seasons it is quite common all over Israel. It can then be seen hopping tirelessly around bushes and trees, searching for insects. In the fall it may even feed on the ripe fruits of various maquis bushes and creepers. Its range includes the countries around the Mediterranean, but it is gradually expanding to the eastern Mediterranean countries as well. This warbler resembles the Sardinian Warbler (which we encountered among the resident birds), but is larger and less graceful. Its yellow eyes are distinctive.

Upcher's Warbler nests near Orphean Warblers, and is best seen in the northern Golan and in the foothills of Mount Hermon. This Warbler has an Irano-Turanian range, from Israel, Lebanon and south-eastern Turkey in the west to Afghanistan and Turkestan in the east. Its brownish-pink legs distinguish it from the Olivaceous Warbler, whose legs are grayish.

Another bird which returns to Israel's maquis areas as well as to olive groves and parklands is the **Masked Shrike**. This small, delicate Shrike

Masked Shrike, *Lanius nubicus*

has a rusty orange tinge on the front of its body. It usually wags its long, narrow tail while perching on regular observation points on top of trees and bushes. Its range is limited to the region between Greece and the coasts of Turkey and the northern tip of the Persian Gulf. During migration seasons, it is quite noticeable in Israel's Negev.

Upcher's Warbler, *Hippolais languida*

Black-headed Bunting, *Emberiza melanocephala*

Unlike all the other summer residents of Israel, which winter in Africa, the **Black-headed Bunting** winters in northwestern India. This Bunting ranges over the eastern Mediterranean and the Irano-Turanian zones. During migration seasons it is visible all over Israel, but it nests mainly in the hill areas in the northern and central parts of the country. It is especially common in the mountains of Galilee, the northern Golan and the foothills of Mount Hermon.

Black-headed Buntings are fond of sparse maquis areas and fruit-tree orchards. In spring they often perch atop a tall tree or a fence-post, singing. The song of the Black-headed Bunting differs from that of other Buntings: it is strong and melodious. The female is colored an unobtrusive olive-brown, while the male, with bright colors in the spring, goes through an interesting moult: it changes part of its feathers as early as June or July, taking on a rather drab appearance. Another moult and color change occurs during the winter. However, its conspicuous coloring persists under the other feathers. As the paler-colored feathers wear away in the course of the winter, the bright colors reappear.

The **Bee-eater** is probably the most colorful and noticeable of Israel's birds. It is also recognized by its loud whistling calls which are audible at a distance: Bee-eaters can easily be heard before they are seen. During migration, communicating calls between Bee-eaters can even be heard at night. Bee-eaters are gregarious, migrating in bands and nesting in colonies. The nests are in burrows which the bird excavates in vertical river banks. Some colonies number dozens of nest openings side by side.

The Bee-eater is the only member of its family apart from the Blue-cheeked Bee-eater, which has spread beyond Africa and penetrated throughout Europe. It is fond of bees, and a band attacking a beehive can destroy it. However, it is worth noting that Bee-eaters also feed on wasps, which cause considerable damage to beehives; thus, the birds can offset the damage they cause.

Bee-eater, *Merops apiaster*

The **Great Spotted Cuckoo** also comes from tropical Africa. Outside Africa, it is found in the Iberian peninsula, southern France, western Italy, Turkey, Cyprus and Israel. Like many other species of its family, it, too, is a parasite. In Israel, the hooded crow is its main and almost sole host. Great Spotted Cuckoos will rarely lay their eggs in the nests of Brown-necked Raven. In flight, Great Spotted Cuckoos resemble hawks. They sound loud, hoarse calls on the wing, a feature which inspired their Latin name — *clamator* — which means "screamer".

Great Spotted Cuckoo, *Clamator glandarius*

Collared Pratincole, *Glareda pratincola*

Lesser Kestrel, *Falco naumanii*

Another bird originally from tropical Africa found in southern Europe and western Asia is the **Collared Pratincole**. This gregarious bird lives in fields and open plains, usually near water sources. It feeds on flying insects, performing aerobatic feats as it flies. Nowadays, Collared Pratincoles are quite rare summer visitors in Israel. They prefer to nest in plowed fields, often adopting fields of cotton which have just sprouted when the birds return from their wintering areas. Field cultivation and the use of various pesticides caused considerable damage to the population of these birds, which declined markedly.

The widespread use of pesticides in agricultural areas during the 1950s and early 1960s had a severe effect on most populations of raptors in Israel, including that of the **Lesser Kestrel**. This bird of prey resembles the Kestrel in coloring, size and behavior, but tends to flock together more during nesting and migration. It returns to Israel from Africa between mid-February and mid-March, and nests mainly during April and May. Lesser Kestrels nest in cliff crevices, but seem to prefer attics of houses. Thus, in the spring of 1990 about 35 pairs nested in the houses of the small farming community of Avi'el, southeast of Zikhron Ya'acov. They abandon their nesting colonies in July, and by the end of August they are on their way back to Africa. These Kestrels feed mainly on insects which they catch in open areas and cultivated fields. These feeding grounds are also where they consumed the pesticides. Lesser Kestrels have a Mediterranean — Irano-Turanian range.

Another raptor seriously affected by pesticides is the **Egyptian Vulture**. This bird was used as a symbol in the hieroglyphics of ancient Egypt, hence its name.

Egyptian Vultures are carrion-eaters, but they also enjoy feeding on garbage. During the 1980s, dozens of Egyptian Vultures gathered every morning in spring and summer on the garbage dump of Sdeh Boker in the northern Negev.

Egyptian Vultures are distributed throughout the savanna zone of tropical Africa, as well as in northern Africa, southern Europe, southwestern Asia and India. The more northerly populations of Egyptian Vulture pass through Israel's skies on migration. Only a small proportion passes over Eilat. They are more common along the shore of the Dead Sea; a hundred Egyptian Vultures can be seen there in a single day.

Egyptian Vultures nest in cliff crevices. The clutch usually consists of two eggs. Incubation lasts for 41 days, and the chick leaves the nest at the age of 75 days.

Egyptian Vulture, *Neophron percnopterus*

WINTERING BIRDS

Even people who are not avid bird enthusiasts find it difficult to remain indifferent to the wintering birds. Before winter, members of about 100 bird species arrive in Israel, mainly from Europe but also from central and northern Asia. Some of these are small and shy, such as Accentors, Black Redstarts or Chiffchaffs. Others are large and noisy, gathering in flocks that can number thousands, hundreds of thousands or even millions. Among the latter are Starlings and Black-headed Gulls.

Some wintering birds are harmless, such as Wagtails, Chaffinches, and Sandpipers. Others spread over cultivated fields, and farmers would be glad to be rid of them because of the damage they cause to crops. This damage can be major: Skylarks peck at sprouts in grainfields and vegetable patches, while the Cormorant exhibits its fishing prowess in fishponds, where it prefers carp to other species.

Some birds winter close to home, and even maintain their territories throughout the season. Among these are Wagtails, Robins and Black Redstarts. Stonechats have permanent territories in fields, but most field birds wander in flocks: among these are Lapwings, Rooks, Jackdaws and Cranes. However, most of the action during winter concentrates around fishponds, such as those of Ma'agan Mikha'el. The Hula Nature Reserve is another favorite area. As many as 100 different species of water birds can be seen in such locations: various Ducks, Plovers, Sandpipers, Coots, Herons, and many others.

Some of the wintering birds arrive early and can be observed from August. Among these are the Kingfisher, Herring Gull and Gray Heron. Others linger in Israel until April: Great Crested Grebe, Shoveler, Black Kite and Wagtail. However, most of the wintering birds arrive and stay in Israel during December-January.

Black Kite, *Milvuss migrans*

Black-headed Gull, *Larus ridibundus*

One of the most noticeable wintering birds is the **Black-headed Gull**. Although it is not the most numerous species, it is easily observed. Thousands of them gather on every garbage dump all over Israel. These birds live along seas, rivers and lakes, and feed on garbage and waste products. At the same time, they congregate in large numbers in fishponds. During the afternoon, they begin returning to their roosting spots along the Mediterranean and the Sea of Galilee. They pass through Israel's skies every evening in arrow formation. In the morning they return to the garbage dumps, where they encounter **Black Kites**. This raptor is also fond of feeding on garbage. At the Hadera dump near the coastal road, for example, dozens of Kites can be seen gliding over the garbage heaps, navigating by twisting and turning the edges of their long tails. There are also many at the western Negev garbage dump, near Kibbutz Tze'elim, and in the Hula valley.

Starling, *Sturmus vulgaris*

Sociable Plover, *Chettusia gregaria*

Not far from the kites in the western Negev **Cranes** are also visible. Hundreds and even thousands of Cranes gather. Their calls carry over great distances, even when they themselves are too far away to be seen.

Cranes can also be seen and heard in other parts of the country, mainly in the Hula Valley. At dusk, some 3000 Cranes gather in the Hula Reserve to spend the night. During the day they scatter around the fields, feeding on the remnants of peanut and cotton plants.

Sprouting grainfields are also the best place to see flocks of Rooks, Jackdaws, and mainly **Starlings**. These devour shoots, wheat grains and even feed on tiny animals. In recent years Starlings have discovered the high nutritive value of the food pellets fed to cows, sheep and chickens. They arrive in masses to share the feed of these domestic animals. Hundreds of thousands, and even millions, of Starlings can assemble on these occasions. The farming settlements of the southern Golan are especially susceptible to these attacks. A sudden noise sends aloft a black cloud over the settlement, and a rain of white droppings descends.

Their twilight maneuvers around their roosting sites are spectacular. No choreographer could achieve such perfection in a dance troupe. The "troupe" in this case numbers tens of thousands of "dancers". However, the exact location of such a roosting colony is hard to determine, since it may change. Sometimes colonies develop in big cities such as Tel Aviv or Jerusalem. The Starlings of the western

Negev usually roost among the reeds and tamarisk trees in Nahal HaBessor or Nahal Gerar.

In the fields of the western Negev, another bird worth spotting is the **Sociable Plover**. This rather large Plover nests in a limited area: the grassy plains of the central and southern USSR. Most of its population winters in northwestern India and Sudan. Sociable Plovers are rare winterers in most of Israel's area, but are quite common in the western Negev. They can sometimes be seen in numbers of 100 or more. When it is in the air, it is unmistakeable, with its tri-colored wings: sandy-beige, black and white.

Spotted Redshank, *Tringa erythropus*

However, most Plovers can be seen in the fishponds and along the Mediterranean shore. Some 25 members of this large family can be seen in these regions. Knowing and identifying them is a favorite challenge for birdwatchers. We have chosen to present the **Spotted Redshank** as a representative of the Plover family. It nests mainly in Siberia and the far north. Its winter plumage is predominantly a light gray. At that season, it is distinguished by its long red legs and its long bill. In summer, its plumage is very dark; most of the feathers are black. The Spotted Redshank ventures into deeper waters than the other Plovers, and is fond of swimming. Swimming is usually done in a crowded group.

Crane, *Grus grus*

Great White Egret, *Egretta alba*

As they wander along the edges of the fishponds, mainly those recently drained of water in order to remove the fish for marketing, Plovers may encounter Herons. Israel's resident Herons, such as Little Egret, Squacco Heron and Night Heron, are joined by hundreds of **Great White Egrets** and Gray Herons. The censuses of Israel's Nature Reserve Authority show that about 1200 Great White Egrets and 6200 Gray Herons spend the winter in Israel each year. During the day they scatter over the fishponds. One or two fish a day satisfy them; they spend the rest of the time motionless. In the Hula Valley they also catch voles in the fields. At dusk, they gather to spend the night.

Most of the Herons of Israel's coastal plain flock to eucalyptus trees near Caesarea. The Herons of the Hula Valley gather in the Hula Nature Reserve.

Thousands of **Cormorants** also assemble every evening in the Hula Reserve. In the morning, they fly to the Sea of Galilee, 25 km away, at speeds of about 70 km per hour. They scatter in the area and catch fish. In the afternoon they return to the reserve: wave after wave of Cormorants

Ruddy Shelduck, *Tadorna ferruginea*

arrives, in arrowhead formation. All the birds land on a few trees in the reserve, to spend the night. This takes place daily from early November to the end of March. Hundreds of Cormorants also attempt to spend the winter in the coastal plain, but fish-growers drive them off, understandably. Thus, Cormorants spend most of their day flying around in search of a suitable spot.

Fish-growers are more tolerant of the Ducks which winter at the fishponds, and justly so. These only strain out and consume algae, seeds, lower crustaceans and small aquatic insects. About 25 species of ducks have been identified in Israel. Only three of these species breed in this country; the others are winterers or accidentals. Ten of the latter can be considered common, or even very common. The others are rare or very rare. One of Israel's very rare wintering species is the **Shelduck**. In some years, no more than 15 individuals can be seen in all the country's reservoirs. There have been years when over 2000 individuals were counted. Even rarer is the **Ruddy Shelduck**. This large Duck is noticeable from afar with its rusty chestnut coloring. The Ruddy Shelduck's range extends through arid regions from Morocco and Turkey, through the southern USSR and Afghanistan, to Mongolia.

Shelduck, *Tadorna tadorna*

As winter nears, it begins to roam, and a large part of its population spends the winter in rice fields in India and southeastern Asia. According to some reports, it used to nest in Israel, but there is no clear evidence of this. Nowadays, at any rate, it is only a rare winterer.

Cormorant, *Phalacrocorax carbo*

Another very rare winterer is the **Great Black-headed Gull**. This large, ungainly Gull has a distinctive large, thick bill. Its range lies between the northern part of the Black Sea and central Asia. Most of its populations spend the winter along the shores of southern Asia, from the Persian Gulf to Vietnam. A small proportion winters in the Red Sea. In Israel, Great Black-headed Gulls winter mainly at the coast of Mount Carmel and in the nearby fishponds, although they also appear at the Sea of Galilee and in the Hula Valley. This aggressive Gull feeds mostly on fish, and sometimes attacks Gulls and other water birds to rob them of their prey.

Great Black-headed Gull, *Larus ichthyaetus*

MIGRANT BIRDS

Most bird species of Europe, as well as of central and western Asia, winter in Africa. Many of these pass through Israel on their migration to and from their wintering sites. This group of birds numbers some 120 species, among them the Rose-colored Starling which winters in India and migrates from west to east and back again.

Many of the birds use different routes for their fall and spring migrations. Thus, some species are more noticeable during the fall migration. Among them are Avocet, Gray Plover, Red-footed Falcon, and Lesser Gray Shrike. Others, like Stork, Roller, Pied Flycatcher and Red-headed Shrike, are more conspicuous during the spring migration. The migration of Quail is especially well-known. In the fall, Quails fly across the eastern basin of the Mediterranean Sea in the course of a single night. They then land exhausted on the shores of northern Sinai. In spring, they move north along the full width of Israel.

Stork, *Ciconia ciconia*

The most conspicuous bird migrating through Israel in the spring is undoubtedly the **Stork**. Flocks numbering hundreds of birds, or even thousands, can be seen circling as they rise on a thermal air current, gliding northwards, or landing to feed and to rest. Weaker Storks which lag behind are then observed over most of the country, mainly in plains and valleys: the western Negev, the coastal plain, the Jezreel Valley and the Hula Valley. Storks are less noticeable during the fall migration. At that season they migrate over the eastern watershed of the country. The rate of their fall migration is accelerated, with less laggards.

In the fall the migration of **Pelicans** is the most marked. Untrained observers may mistake Pelicans for Storks: both species are gregarious, large, and glide through the air. They are white, with black primaries. However, despite these similarities, they can easily be told apart even at a distance, when the long legs of the Stork cannot be seen. Pelicans migrate in well-arranged and organized formations — an arrowhead, or a staggered line. As they rise on a thermal current, they carry out the turns in unison. Storks, on the other hand, seem to migrate together, but actually migrate individually, with hardly any connection or dependence on the others.

The best and most convenient place to watch Pelicans is in the Hula Reserve. During the second half of October and during most of November, flocks of Pelicans land there almost daily, in groups that may number as many as 3000 individuals. They usually spend one night there and are on their way the next morning.

Many raptor species glide over Israel in the course of their migration. The most prominent and numerous of these, in the fall as well as in the spring, is the **Honey Buzzard**. One year, about half a million Honey Buzzards were counted.

Pelican, *Pelecanus onocrotalus*

Honey Buzzard, *Pernis apivorus*

Yellow Wagtail, *Motacilla flava feldegg*

The fall migration of Honey Buzzards begins at the end of August, and is concentrated mainly in the second week of September. At that time as many as 100,000 individuals can be seen in a single day. In the fall, they migrate mostly over the western slopes of Israel's hill regions. In the spring, they are the last raptors to migrate. The best region for watching them in spring is around Eilat. Their spring migration lasts mainly from mid-April to mid-May. Sometimes, they are so weak and exhausted that they can be approached quite closely.

Songbirds also arrive at Eilat in a state of exhaustion. Many of them are so thirsty that they nearly lose their sense of fear when they are near the water.

The **Yellow Wagtail** has a wide range, covering most of Europe and Asia. About 15 different subspecies of Yellow Wagtails have been described in this area. The subspecies differ from each other mainly in the head coloring of the males during the nesting period. During thc migration season, five subspecies can be seen in Israel. Members of the different subspecies often mingle as they roam the fields and water bodies, searching for insects.

The first subspecies to appear during migration seasons, in fall as well as in spring, is the black-headed *M. feldegg*. This subspecies is limited to the region between the Balkans and Afghanistan. A few pairs formerly nested in the Hula Valley swamps, before these were drained.

While it is simple to identify the males of the different subspecies of Yellow Wagtail in their summer habit, the females are almost indistinguishable from each other. Their color is more faded. The female Red-throated Pipit is also drab and less conspicuous than the male. This Pipit has an Arctic range: from northern Scandinavia to the Bering Straits. It is quite a common winterer in moist fields, but is especially noticeable as a common migrant. It migrates in small groups. The main part of its fall migration occurs in October and November, and in the spring — between the end of March and the end of April. Its throat and breast take on a distinctive reddish tone closer to summer, after a partial moult.

Blue-cheeked Bee-eater, *Merops superciliosus.*

Isabelline Wheatear, *Oenanthe oenanthe*

Unlike the Yellow Wagtail and the Red-throated Pipit, the males and females of the **Isabelline Wheatear** cannot be told apart on the basis of feathering. There is no seasonal difference in feathering, either; and the young birds resemble the adults. The Isabelline Wheatear is a large Wheatear, its general coloring a rather uniform sandy-brown. Like most other Wheatears, it has a marked "black flag" at the tip of its white tail. Its range lies between Turkey and central China. It is quite a common nester in the southern and central Golan, and a very rare winterer in the fields of the western Negev. However, during the migration seasons (August — October, and from late February to early April) it is noticeable in all the open areas of Israel.

The **Greater Sand-plover** has a similar range, but it can be seen in Israel almost exclusively along the Mediterranean shore and the Gulf of Eilat. This is a large plover, with a distinctive bill which is longer than that of other plover species.

The last migrant on our list, which has an Asian range — from southeastern Turkey to the central USSR — is the **Blue Cheeked Bee-eater** (a similar species is found in tropical Africa). This Bee-eater differs from the commoner bee-eater not only in its color, which is almost entirely green, but also in its longer bill and greater agility in flight. It sometimes migrates in mixed flocks with Bee-eaters.

Greater Sand-plover,
Charadrius leschenautii

VAGRANT BIRDS

Israel has about 120 species of vagrant birds. This number has greatly increased in recent years, thanks to the rising number of nature enthusiasts as well as to the creation of new habitats. The final count is probably yet to come, and more surprises are certainly in store. Some of these vagrants, like Flamingo, appear almost every year, but unpredictably as to time and place. Others were observed in Israel only once, such as White-capped Albatross which nests in southern Australia and southern New Zealand, and usually roams the regions south of the Tropic of Capricorn.

About one-quarter of the vagrants are Arctic species, which usually winter at the water bodies of southern Europe, far to the north of Israel. Among these are Black-throated Diver, Slavonian Grebe, Whooper Swan, and Long-tailed Duck. During extremely cold winters, these birds may be impelled south of their usual haunts. Other species which are common throughout Europe are irruptive. When their populations suddenly expand, they may stray into Israel, sometimes in considerable numbers. Among these are Crossbill, Hawfinch, and Siskin.

Some vagrants are species which nest throughout Asia and winter in southern Asia or in Africa, and have strayed far away from their normal route. These include Olive-backed Pipit, Citrine Wagtail, Radde's Warbler and Dusky Thrush.

Other vagrants are tropical species, such as Goliath Heron, Yellow-billed Stork, Cape Teal, Kittlitz's Sand-plover, Gray-headed Gull, and even raptors such as Black Eagle or Black-shouldered Kite.

Finally, vagrants also include sea birds such as Leach's Petrel, Gannet, and Shag.

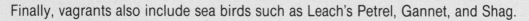

Citrine Wagtail, *Motacilla citreola*

46

Striated Scops Owl,
Otus brucei

A rare vagrant from the Siberian tundras is Red-breasted Goose, a small, colorful member of its family. It is a rare winterer along the shores of the Black Sea and in the delta of the Tigris and Euphrates rivers. It has been observed several times in Israel. Red-breasted Geese often feed in fields, usually with White-fronted Goose.

Richard's Pipit originates in the region between southwestern Siberia and the Altai mountains in eastern Kazakhstan. It usually winters in eastern Asia and tropical Africa (where other subspecies related to it are resident). It occurs in Israel as a rare vagrant; it is a bit more common in the southern Arava and Eilat regions. This large, light-colored Pipit has a long tail and legs, and a distinctive erect bearing. The claw of the hind finger is very long and only slightly curved.

Citrine Wagtails usually winter in India and southeastern Asia. During the nesting season, the male's head and belly are yellow, while the upper mantle is black. These colors are unmistakeable. During the rest of the year, the male — like the female and the young bird — resembles several other subspecies of Yellow Wagtail, and can be mistakenly identified. In recent years it has been increasingly observed, mainly in the Eilat region, but also in the coastal region, such as the fishponds of Ma'agan Mikha'el and slightly further north. It sometimes spends quite some time in one area during the winter.

The main range of the **Striated Scops Owl** is between Iraq and southern Iran and the Sea of Aral; however, there is an isolated enclave in the southern part of Saudi Arabia as well. Because of its resemblance to the Scops Owl, it is quite difficult to identify in the field. On the whole, it has a grayer tone, lighter colors (especially on the face) and more delicate markings on its breast.

Israel's vagrant Flamingoes originate in Lake Romiya, in northwestern Iraq. Four rings found on the legs of dead individuals are proof of this. Vagrants in Israel are usually young, grayish birds. However, adult Flamingoes in full color occasionally appear. They then prefer to stay in the salt ponds of Eilat, and may stray to the salt ponds at Atlit. Occasionally they may be seen in fishponds throughout Israel.

The head of the Gulf of Eilat is one of the best places for spotting vagrants in Israel. This is where the white-capped Albatross was found, as well as Black-throated Diver and Long-tailed Duck. From time to time, a few Gannets are seen, as well as several species of tropical sea birds.

One of these is **Western Reef Heron**. This Heron has two habits: white, and slate-gray. The white habit, the commonest in this region, is very similar to that of the Little Egret, except for the yellow bill and the pale-yellow iris. This Egret nests on mangrove trees in southern Sinai. It feeds mainly on fish, sometimes walking over coral reefs. Often, it spreads its wings to shade the surface. One explanation is that this shading is a method of attracting fish.

Another vagrant, whose world range is limited to the Red Sea and its close vicinity, is **White-eyed Gull**. It is quite common along the coasts of southern Sinai and Tiran Island, where it also sometimes nests. It is a rare vagrant at the head of the Gulf of Eilat. White-eyed Gulls, too, feed mainly on fish; but on the coasts of Sinai they sometimes penetrate into the desert to a distance of as much as one km. There the bird hovers around common nitraria bushes, picking off the orange fruits.

The **Namaqua Dove** comes from tropical Africa and southwestern Arabia. This small, delicate Dove has a very long tail. The male's cheeks, forehead and throat are black. Namaqua Doves now seem to have become resident in the southern Arava, and can be observed from time to time in other parts of the country.

White-eyed Gull, *Larus leucophthalmus*

Lesser Crested Terns also nest on Tiran Island, and are vagrants at the head of the Gulf of Eilat. It is a very rare vagrant on the shore of the Mediterranean. This medium-sized Tern is identified by its orange bill and black legs. It is an agile flyer, and enjoys resting on the water. It feeds almost exclusively on small fish.